All About Cheetahs

EDventure
LEARNING

How to Use This Book

This book is part of our Read Together series, a collection of books designed to be enjoyed by a young reader paired with a more experienced reader, such as a parent, grandparent, or older sibling. Take turns reading out loud together.

The pages on the left side are meant for the younger reader. These pages use short, simple sentences and larger print. They are marked at the bottom of the page with the symbol shown at left.

The right-side pages are for the older reader. They contain paragraphs with longer sentences and more complex vocabulary. These pages are marked at the bottom of the page with the symbol shown at right.

Shared reading helps new readers gain confidence. It's also a great way for all ages to bond over books. We hope you enjoy this book as you Read Together.

Printed in the United States of America
Paperback ISBN: 978-1-64824-015-7

EDventure Learning LLC
5601 State Route 31 #1296
Clay, NY 13039

www.edventurelearning.com
Email us at hello@edventurelearning.com

Table of Contents

What Cheetahs Look Like

They are big cats.

Cheetahs are part of the big cat family. They are one of the smaller animals in this group, however. Tigers, lions, leopards, and panthers are all larger than cheetahs.

An average adult cheetah is 2-3 feet (0.6-0.9 m) tall and 3.5-5 feet (1-1.5m) long (not including the tail). Adult cheetahs usually weigh between 75 and 145 pounds (34 and 66 kg).

They have spots.

Cheetahs have yellow fur with small black spots. Each cheetah's spot pattern is unique. All cheetahs also have black streaks of fur that stretch from their eyes to their mouths. These "tear marks" actually help to keep the sun's glare out of their eyes, making it easier for them to see to hunt.

Their tails have stripes.

A cheetah's tail is 2-3 feet (0.6-0.9 m) long. The tail has fluffy fur with the same spotted pattern as the rest of the body except for the end, which is striped. A cheetah's tail is wider and flatter than the tails of other big cats. This helps the cheetah steer while running quickly.

They have big paws.

A cheetah's rear paws are larger than its front paws, which helps it to take off quickly to run. Cheetahs have claws on their paws. Unlike the claws of most big cats, cheetahs' claws do not retract. That means they always stick out of the paws. The claws dig into the ground, helping cheetahs keep their balance when running and turning quickly. Cheetahs also use their claws for hunting, eating, and climbing.

Where Cheetahs Live

Most cheetahs live in Africa.

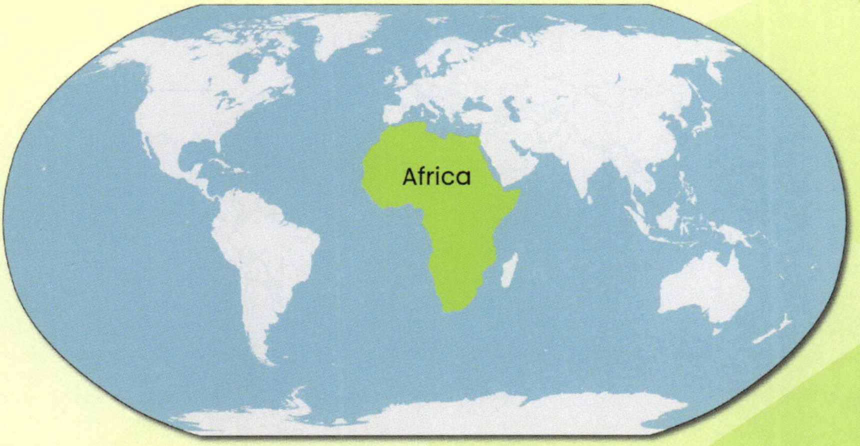

Nearly all cheetahs live in the African **savanna**- large plains with tall grass and scattered trees. A small number of cheetahs live in the Middle East.

They live in open spaces.

Cheetahs live in wide, flat plains with lots of room to run. Cheetahs' coats help them blend in with the tall grass in the savanna.

What Cheetahs Do

They run very fast.

Cheetahs are most famous for their speed. They are the fastest land animals in the world. They can reach top speed of up to 70 miles (112 km) per hour. They can go from 0 to 60 miles per hour in just 3 seconds!

They run in short bursts.

Running at full speed takes a lot of energy, so cheetahs do not usually run for long periods of time. They usually sprint for less than a minute.

They hunt for food.

Cheetahs are **carnivores**, which means they only eat meat. Cheetahs hunt for prey such as gazelles, impalas, warthogs, and hares. They use their speed and excellent vision to help them find and catch their prey.

Cheetahs make many sounds.

Unlike other big cats, cheetahs cannot roar. They use many other noises to communicate. Cheetahs purr, meow, growl, hiss, and even chirp!

They have cubs.

A baby cheetah is called a **cub**. A female cheetah usually gives birth to a litter of 3-5 cubs at a time. Cubs stay with their mother until they are around two years old.

They live in small groups.

Adult males and females spend most of their time apart. Males form small groups called **coalitions** that live and hunt together. A female cheetah lives only with her own cubs.

Glossary

Carnivore

Animal that eats only meat

Coalition

Group of male cheetahs

Cub

Baby cheetah

Savanna

Plains with scattered trees and a warm climate

Index

Credits

The images in this book are used with permission as follows. Images not listed here are © EDventure Learning LLC.

Cover and title page: Pixworld | Dreamstime; Interior backgrounds: Kappy Kappy | Rawpixel; p. 3: David Groves | Unsplash; p. 4: Pixworld | Dreamstime; p. 5: Adogslifephoto | Dreamstime (left), Macrovector | Freepik (right); p. 6: Sophia Hilmer | Pixabay; p. 7: Andy Brunner | Unsplash; p. 8: Bing Bing Zhu | Dreamstime; p. 9: Nadine Trief | Pixabay; p. 10: Sommer Rayn | Pixabay; p. 11: Bobby Bradley | Dreamstime (top), Michael M. | Pexels (bottom); p. 12: Jean Wimmerlin | Unsplash; p. 13: Clker Free Vector Images | Pixabay (top); David Clode | Unsplash (bottom); p. 14: Magda Ehlers | Pexels; p. 15: Sutirta Budiman | Unsplash; p. 16: Bob Suir | Dreamstime; p. 17: Dr Zoltan | Pixabay; p. 18: Stu Porter | Dreamstime; p. 19: Charl Durand | Unsplash; p. 20: Michael Aleo | Unsplash; p. 21: Victor Lapaev | Dreamstime; p. 22: Eric Heininger | Unsplash; p. 23: Saad Khan | Unsplash; p. 24: Jean-Daniel Calame | Unsplash; p. 25: Skeeze | Pixabay; p. 26: Ronbd | Pixabay; p. 27: Blacky-63 | Pixabay (top), Carole Henderson | Pixabay (bottom); p. 28 (from top): Michael Aleo | Unsplash, Ronbd | Pixabay, Skeeze | Pixabay, Sutirta Budiman | Unsplash

Check out these other titles in the Read Together series!

All About Camels

All About Cheetahs

All About Giraffes

All About Elephants

All About Kangaroos

Keep in touch!

FOLLOW US ON SOCIAL MEDIA

@edventurelearning

www.edventurelearning.com

Want freebies? Email us at **hello@edventurelearning.com** with the subject "Read Together" to join our newsletter and we'll send you free printables to keep the learning going!

All About Lions

All About Penguins

All About Polar Bears

All About Tigers

All About Zebras

Printed in Poland
by Amazon Fulfillment
Poland Sp. z o.o., Wrocław

90610280R00018